Using Community Policing to Counter Violent Extremism

5 KEY PRINCIPLES FOR LAW ENFORCEMENT

Contents

LETTER FROM THE COPS OFFICE DIRECTOR AND IACP PRESIDENT

Dear colleague,

On behalf of the International Association of Chiefs of Police (IACP) and the Office of Community Oriented Policing Services (COPS Office), we are pleased to present *Using Community Policing to Counter Violent Extremism: Five Key Principles for Law Enforcement,* a guide to using community policing as a front-line strategy to prevent terrorism across the diverse communities served by law enforcement agencies throughout the country. This document provides practical insights and compelling examples of how to extend the principles of community policing in ways that help prevent terrorism and violent extremism while building stronger communities and preserving constitutional and civil rights.

Since the tragic events of the terrorist attacks of September 11, 2001, federal, state, local, and tribal law enforcement have worked to better coordinate response and prevention strategies. The Department of Homeland Security (DHS) has continually adapted its mission to the reality that homeland security *starts with hometown security.*

Whether the motivations for violent extremism are based on a foreign radical ideology or are the product of the "sovereign citizen" belief system, the actions of the violent extremists and the crimes they commit are inherently local. Their plots to carry out attacks, the crimes committed in furtherance of their plans, and the impact of their attacks should they succeed all take place in a local jurisdiction. As executives representing the COPS Office and the IACP, we understand the critical front-line role that local law enforcement plays with respect to terrorism.

As longtime advocates of community policing, we also recognize that local police cannot do their job alone. Local police agencies are in the best position to work closely with local residents, business owners, community groups, and other local stakeholders as vital partners in detecting suspicious activities, preventing acts of terrorism, and building communities that are resilient to violent extremism.

It is clear that community policing approaches that have been used successfully to reduce fear of crime, prevent crime, and improve public safety can be used with equal effectiveness to address and prevent terrorism. Indeed, the same partnership-building strategies that have paid dividends for decades are now being used to improve hometown and homeland security. While progress has been made, we recognize too that not all local agencies are equally aware of and prepared for the critical roles they play in promoting hometown and homeland security.

It is our hope that this guide will help close that gap and enable all agencies to fulfill their critical role in protecting both their communities and our nation.

Sincerely,

Ronald L. Davis, Director
Office of Community Oriented Policing Services

Yousry Zakhary, President
International Association of Chiefs of Police

ACKNOWLEDGMENTS

The International Association of Chiefs of Police (IACP) would like to express its gratitude to the following law enforcement agencies:

- Arlington County (Virginia) Police Department
- City of Fairfax (Virginia) Police Department
- Dearborn (Michigan) Police Department
- Fairfax County (Virginia) Police Department
- Greensboro (North Carolina) Police Department
- Harper College (Illinois) Police Department
- Hennepin County (Minnesota) Sheriff's Office
- Jackson (Tennessee) Police Department
- Los Angeles (California) Police Department
- Los Angeles (California) Sheriff's Department
- Loudoun County (Virginia) Sheriff's Office
- Mankato (Minnesota) Department of Public Safety
- Minneapolis (Minnesota) Police Department
- Montgomery County (Maryland) Police Department
- New York State Police
- Ohio State Highway Patrol
- Prince George's County (Maryland) Police Department
- Royal Canadian Mounted Police
- Saint Paul (Minnesota) Police Department
- Seminole County (Florida) Sheriff's Office
- Utah Department of Public Safety

Representatives from these agencies comprised the majority of the project's advisory group. Some of these representatives also serve on relevant IACP committees—including the Committee on Terrorism, the Civil Rights Committee, and the Community Policing Committee—that helped inform this project. Members of the advisory group provided invaluable input and examples, participated in follow-up interviews and case studies, and hosted site visits. The advisory group was instrumental in informing the development of the deliverables associated with this project. The key principles and many of the examples outlined in this guide were taken directly from these agencies.

The IACP is also grateful for the insight and assistance provided by federal partners throughout the project. The Office of Community Oriented Policing Services (COPS Office) deserves special recognition for their support and continued promotion of the benefits of community oriented policing. In addition to the COPS Office, representatives from The White House and the following agencies were instrumental in assisting with this project:

- National Counterterrorism Center
- U.S. Attorney's Office
- U.S. Department of Homeland Security
- U.S. Department of Justice

EXECUTIVE SUMMARY

The bombing at the Boston Marathon and the killing of two sheriff's deputies in Saint John Parish, Louisiana, by two sovereign citizens demonstrate that violent extremism continues to be a reality in the United States. These incidents help to demonstrate the range of violent ideologies and highlight some of the threats posed by violent extremists nationwide. Communities of all sizes are dealing with individuals and groups that proffer violent interpretations of ideologies, radicals hoping to identify and groom new recruits, and individuals that are radicalizing to violence.

State, local, and tribal (SLT) law enforcement agencies are responding to the threats posed by violent extremism by integrating community oriented policing principles and homeland security. Community policing encourages law enforcement to use partnerships and problem-solving techniques to proactively address public safety concerns. It promotes leveraging the most valuable resource in any community—its members—by building relationships based on understanding, trust, and respect. Community members can further inform law enforcement about their religions, cultures, and beliefs, so that officers are able to distinguish between constitutionally protected and criminal behavior. More important, community members are best positioned to recognize suspicious activities in their communities.

The Federal Government has also incorporated community policing into its countering violent extremism (CVE) strategy. The White House documents *Empowering Local Partners to Prevent Violent Extremism in the United States* and the *Strategic Implementation Plan for Empowering Local Partners to Prevent Violent Extremism in the United States* commit the Federal Government to supporting and empowering local communities and their partners to prevent violent extremism. Also, the Federal Government is helping communities better understand and protect themselves against violent extremist propaganda through improved information sharing about the threat of radicalization and increased cooperation with local law enforcement agencies.

In coordination with the federal strategy, the International Association of Chiefs of Police (IACP), with support from the U.S. Department of Justice (DOJ), Office of Community Oriented Policing Services (COPS Office), created the *Role of Community Policing in Homeland Security and Countering Violent Extremism* project. The goal of this project is to increase the capacity of law enforcement nationwide to develop problem solving strategies to identify, prevent, and eliminate terrorist ideologies and behaviors. This guide was developed as part of the project to serve as a resource for law enforcement organizations considering, planning, and employing community policing practices tailored to countering violent extremism in their communities. The guide details the following five key community policing principles and the roles they play in contributing to homeland security:

Key Principle 1: Foster and Enhance Trusting Partnerships with the Community

Trusting partnerships are the cornerstone of community policing. When based on trust, transparency, respect, and mutual understanding, partnerships can foster a common purpose of keeping communities safe from all types of violent extremism.

Key Principle 2: Engage All Residents to Address Public Safety Matters

Engaging individuals on a broad array of public safety and quality-of-life issues allows individuals and groups to address their concerns. Various subsets of the community may have different priorities. Providing each group with a forum to address their specific grievances, which may also be underlying causes of radicalization to violence, can help community members feel more involved. Engaging residents can be a valuable force multiplier for law enforcement.

Key Principle 3: Leverage Public and Private Stakeholders

Leveraging the strengths of public and private stakeholders allows law enforcement to utilize resources from the entire community, share valuable information across the entire spectrum of services, and increase public recognition and visibility of countering violent extremism initiatives. These stakeholders can also serve as liaisons between law enforcement and their communities.

Key Principle 4: Utilize All Partnerships to Counter Violent Extremism

Serving in a supporting role as educators, facilitators, and representatives of local government, law enforcement agencies can empower all of their partners—community members, public stakeholders, and private companies—to create counter-narratives, build resilience, and counter violent extremism.

Key Principle 5: Train All Members of the Department

Training that complements the fundamental principles and tactics of community policing is necessary to facilitate the successful implementation of community policing. Training should be up to date and unbiased, stress the differences between countering violent extremism and counterterrorism, and be mandatory for all members of the department.

The guide is laid out in four sections. The **Introduction** provides an overview of community policing and the integral role that community policing principles play in countering violent extremism. The second section, **Highlighting the Threat**, details some of the violent extremist threats facing communities nationwide and defines radicalization to violence. Section three, **Key Principles**, details the five key community policing principles and provides examples from agencies nationwide that have successfully implemented the principles to counter violent extremism. The **Conclusion** reiterates the importance of community policing in homeland security and preventing radicalization to violence.

INTRODUCTION

"Countering radicalization to violence is frequently best achieved by engaging and empowering individuals and groups at the local level to build resilience against violent extremism."[1]

In the years since the 9/11 terrorist attacks, state, local, and tribal (SLT) police have become increasingly important in providing for the national security of the United States.[2] To put it simply, "hometown security is homeland security."

Terrorism and other acts of violent extremism begin, and are carried out, at the local level where SLT police are well-equipped to intervene. Even violent acts with national or international dimensions are first responded to by SLT agencies. There are well-known examples of the contacts local law enforcement had with several of the hijackers involved in the 9/11 attacks.[3] Even prior to 9/11, Timothy McVeigh—the perpetrator of the Oklahoma City bombing—was initially stopped by a state trooper for speeding and driving without a valid license plate.[4] He was only detained at the scene for a possible weapons violation and it was not until days later that he was officially named a suspect.[5]

Recognizing terrorism, violent extremism, and precursor crimes as problems that begin at the local level provides SLT police with the ability to address them using the same community policing philosophy that has been instrumental in reducing fear, disorder, and crime over the past few decades. Community policing is a flexible approach to address crime and disorder problems, and has been widely implemented across the United Sates over the last two decades. While there is no standard method to implementing community policing, there are core elements that comprise community policing approaches.

According to the COPS Office, community policing "promotes organizational strategies that support the systematic use of partnerships and problem-solving techniques, to proactively address the immediate conditions that give rise to public safety issues such as crime, social disorder, and fear of crime."[6] The philosophy is composed of three key components: partnerships with the community, organizational transformation, and problem solving.[7] Collaborative partnerships entail working with individuals and relevant community stakeholders to identify and prioritize problems and develop innovative solutions, while increasing public trust in law enforcement. These partnerships include traditional and nontraditional organizations and services and are based on understanding, trust, respect, and the notion that strong partnerships can help address underlying issues that law enforcement alone may not be able to address. Organizational transformation refers to the alignment of agency personnel, structure, and infrastructure to support the philosophy of community policing. Community policing involves refocusing agency processes and resources from the traditional reactive policing model of responding to calls, to a proactive model that is driven by addressing community concerns before they become larger problems. This change is generally accompanied by decentralizing the command structure, decision making, and accountability; the long-term assignment of officers to specific neighborhoods or beats; and, a focus on increasing effectiveness and efficiency.[8] Finally, problem solving involves engaging in the systematic examination of priorities identified by the community in order to develop responses and evaluate their implementation.[9]

For more information on improving the public's awareness and reporting of suspicious activity, see these two IACP/FEMA publications: *Improving the Public's Awareness and Reporting of Suspicious Activity: Key Research Findings* and *A Resource Guide to Improve Your Community's Awareness and Reporting of Suspicious Activity: For Law Enforcement and Community Partners*. For more information about the NSI, visit http://nsi.ncirc.gov/.

Applying Community Policing to Homeland Security Issues

Community policing approaches have been adapted to address a broad range of concerns. Besides traditional crime issues, community policing has been used to address diverse issues such as gangs and gang violence, civic engagement, and community awareness. Community policing's broad approach encompasses greater emphasis on proactive and preventive policing.

Applying the same community policing principles that have helped reduce general crime, violence, and social disorder to terrorism and violent extremism can also aid in preventing future attacks. Building partnerships with public and private community stakeholders, interacting with residents and community leaders, sharing information, and investigating reports of suspicious or unusual behavior are all components of community policing that are easily transferable to terrorism prevention and countering violent extremism.[10] Interacting with residents and other community stakeholders can help law enforcement identify and engage citizen groups as partners to address community grievances that may lead to violent extremism. Building trusting relationships based on interaction and collaboration may also lead to increased reporting of suspicious activity as well as sharing of information, target hardening, and improved coordination.[11] Especially in a time of shrinking budgets and increasing expectations for law enforcement agencies, one of the most beneficial aspects of community policing is the principle of leveraging the strength of communities and their members.

Community members are an important force multiplier. They can help identify, prevent, and eliminate terrorist ideologies and behaviors before violence occurs. The importance of individual community members is embodied in the Nationwide Suspicious Activity Reporting (SAR) Initiative (NSI), which encourages individuals to take an active role in reporting any type of suspicious or criminal activity to authorities. During his 2011 State of the Union address, President Barack Obama called on American law enforcement and their communities to continue to work together to stop homegrown violent extremists before their plans become operational:

"Thanks to our intelligence and law enforcement professionals, we're disrupting plots and securing our cities and skies. And as extremists try to inspire acts of violence within our borders, we are responding with the strength of our communities..."[12]

By empowering communities to take an active role in ensuring their safety, law enforcement is well positioned to take a central role in preventing terrorism and countering violent extremism.

Engaging Immigrant Communities through Community Policing

Law enforcement agencies nationwide have used community policing principles to build bridges with immigrant communities that may be wary of law enforcement because of past experiences in their home country.[13] Law enforcement agencies have also used these principles, and continue to use them today, to demonstrate their commitment to balancing the needs of protecting their communities while also protecting individuals from hate crimes and civil rights and liberties violations. However, groups that share, or have been perceived to share, the national background or religions of the perpetrators of the 9/11 attacks may still be hesitant to share tips and may be cautious about partnering with law enforcement. This hesitancy can only be overcome by building trusting relationships, being transparent, and communicating with community members, regardless of their citizenship or immigration status.

The principles of community policing extend beyond the residents of a specific community and encompass working in partnership with other government agencies, public and private stakeholders, and faith- and community-based organizations. For example, enhanced information exchange between local, state, tribal, and federal law enforcement and homeland security partners; improved partnerships between federal, state, and local officials; information sharing between law enforcement and private entities; and, advances in communications technology and interoperable databases, can all be used to address terrorism and violent extremism.[14] Using interoperable databases and sharing information with nonprofits and the private sector provides law enforcement with additional opportunities to prevent violent attacks by extremist individuals and groups.

Case Study: Importance of Partnerships and Information Sharing

The case of Khalid Ali-M Aldawsari exemplifies the importance of partnerships and information sharing between private businesses and law enforcement. Aldawsari had attempted to purchase a toxic chemical that can also be used to make an explosive from a company in North Carolina.* Officials from the company were suspicious that an individual would need the quantity Aldawsari ordered. Additionally, the shipping address was that of a freight company in Texas. The chemical company reported the purchase to the local FBI office in Greensboro, North Carolina. The freight company also contacted the Lubbock (Texas) Police Department after receiving a call from Aldawsari. During the call, he indicated that a package would be arriving and requested that the company hold the package until he could pick it up. Employees were also suspicious because Aldawsari had no previous relationship of any kind with the company. The Lubbock Police Department shared the information with the local branch of the FBI in Dallas. Recognizing this was the second time an FBI office had been contacted regarding Aldawsari, a Joint Terrorism Task Force (JTTF) in Dallas composed of federal, state, local, and campus partners opened an investigation.†

Aldawsari later tried to order chemicals from a company in Georgia, but that company was also suspicious that an individual was ordering a large quantity of chemicals and wanted them shipped to an apartment. They contacted Aldawsari and indicated that they could not ship the chemicals to an apartment because of hazmat restrictions. Combined with enrollment information provided by two universities Aldawsari was connected with—one as a former student and one as a current student—the JTTF was able to establish that Aldawsari was not a student at the university he claimed to be enrolled at and was no longer conducting research that would require the chemicals he was attempting to purchase, and his plot was foiled.‡ Aldawsari was convicted by a federal jury in June 2012 of one count of attempted use of a weapon of mass destruction and sentenced to life in prison. Thanks to the awareness of the individuals, the partnerships between private businesses and law enforcement agencies, and the partnerships between law enforcement agencies, Aldawsari's plot was successfully foiled.

---

* "Khalid Aldawsari Complaint Affidavit," The Washington Post, 2011, retrieved July 5, 2013, http://www.washingtonpost.com/wp-srv/world/documents/khalid-aldawsari-complaint-affidavit.html.

† Ibid.

‡ Ibid.

HIGHLIGHTING THE THREAT

"I do not think this nation has ever faced a more fluid, more dynamic, or more complex terrorism threat. We are seeing an increase in the sources of terrorism, a wider array of terrorism targets, a greater cooperation among terrorist groups, and an evolution in terrorist tactics and communication methodology."[15]

Acts of violent extremism negatively affect communities across the United States. According to the Global Terrorism Database, at least one terrorist attack occurred in each of the 50 states and Puerto Rico between 1970 and 2011.[16] While more than 2,600 total attacks occurred during that time period, only about 200 took place after 2001, with domestic extremist groups being responsible for most of the attacks.[17] While not all of the attacks included fatalities, these statistics help demonstrate the diversity of the threat of violent extremism and the need for the continued persistence of law enforcement agencies and communities nationwide.

Homegrown violent extremists, foreign fighters, and domestic extremists continue to evolve and contribute to the threat that faces law enforcement agencies of all sizes. Individuals and groups within each of these categories are extremely diverse, as are their justifications and targets. Homegrown violent extremists are citizens or long-term residents of a Western country who have rejected Western cultural values, beliefs, and norms in favor of a violent ideology and intend to commit acts of terrorism in Western countries or against their interests overseas.[18] Approximately 70 percent of individuals "arrested, indicted, or otherwise identified" as being involved in attempted terrorism plots between 9/11 and 2010 were United States citizens—either born or naturalized—and even more were legal permanent residents.[19] Foreign fighters are individuals— especially individuals from Western countries—who are recruited to travel abroad to train and fight with a particular extremist group based on the belief that the conflict is politically, ideologically, or religiously justi- fied and that they have a divine obligation to engage in violence.[20] Often, the training and extremist ideology are brought back to the United States to radicalize Americans with similar views and justify acts of violence here. Meanwhile, domestically-radicalized individuals are citizens or long-term residents of a country whose primary social influence has been the cultural values and beliefs of their country of current residence.[21] These individuals include anti-federalists, fundamentalists, political extremists, and sovereign citizens.

Sovereign citizens are a highly conspiracy-oriented group of individuals. Adherents to this ideology believe that the Federal Government is a conspiracy to collect money from citizens and that it has overstepped its jurisdiction.[22] Therefore, these individuals attempt to opt out of their United States citizenship and deny the authority of the government to tax them, issue licenses, issue other official identifying documents such as Social Security cards and numbers, and enact laws and policies. As a result, some sovereign citizens refuse to recognize the authority of police to enforce laws and believe that the local elected sheriff is the only legitimate law enforcement officer in the nation. Generally, the crimes of sovereign citizens are nonviolent and include manufacturing of fraudulent license plates and identifying documents, tax evasion, and mortgage and banking fraud. During traffic stops they may film their interactions with officers, produce a "Public Servant Question- naire" that asks for information that they can then use to blackmail officers, and threaten to file liens and law- suits in an effort to overwhelm law enforcement. However, beyond these minor infractions, some sovereign citizens' interactions with law enforcement have become contentious, and even deadly. In 2010, two officers from West Memphis, Arkansas, were killed by a father and son who adhered to sovereign ideology. Two years later, in August 2012, two deputies in Saint John Parish, Louisiana, were shot and killed by sovereigns.[23] Other officers from Washington, Nevada, Virginia, New Hampshire, and North Carolina have encountered sovereigns during routine shifts, exemplifying the widespread threat potential posed to law enforcement nationwide.

The targets of violent extremist attacks are just as diverse as the ideologies and are not limited to "spectacu-lar," high-casualty attacks. Instead, plotters identify "soft targets" in open areas that offer the ability to get in and out easily. Soft targets are generally fixed locations or structures that hold a large number of unprotected civilians or symbolize economic prosperity, religious freedom, and business. These targets include shop-ping malls and movie theaters, bars and restaurants, schools, places of worship, office buildings and business districts, stadiums and other large venues, and hotels. From 2001 to 2011, the most common targets of terrorists in the United States were businesses and private citizens and property.[24] An increasing number of attacks have also targeted military recruitment centers because they tend to be less secure than military bases. Personnel at these centers and other off-duty military personnel have also become popular targets because they tend to be unarmed and may be less expectant. They also have a symbolic meaning for those groups with anti-American sentiments. By expanding their interests to include smaller-scale attacks against political, economic, symbolic, and infrastructure targets, these individuals and groups have adopted the mentality that staging a successful attack doesn't depend on size.[25] This increase in potential targets requires that communi-ties and law enforcement agencies remain vigilant.

Radicalization to Violence

Radicalization to violence (radicalization) is the process by which individuals are introduced to an overt-ly ideological message and belief system that encourages movement from moderate, mainstream beliefs toward extreme views.[26] These extreme views generally include the fact that engagement in, or facilitation of, violence to achieve social, religious, or polit-ical change is both necessary and justified. Generally, these views are grounded in a radical interpretation of either religious doctrines or the Constitution.

The First Amendment to the U.S. Constitution protects the freedoms of speech, press, religion, and as-sembly. It is important to remember that extremism and radicalization themselves are not crimes. As long as individuals and groups do not partake in, or facilitate, acts of violence or crimes, even those who possess or espouse the most heinous of views must be protected.

Radicalization is an individualized and personal process. The factors that influence a specific individual can change within that individual depending on time or cir-cumstance. The factors that influence the radicalization process differ from person to person, as does the radicalization process itself. Individuals can move back and forth between stages or remain static as factors and levels interact and influence one another. In many cases, the Internet plays an integral role in providing access to information and communication with like-minded individuals that facilitates and complements the offline radicalization process. Other individuals are able to self-radicalize using just the Internet, with their online interactions taking the place of those they would have in a physical environment — e.g., chat rooms and videos taking the place of attendance at meetings.

The Role of the Internet in Radicalization to Violence and Violent Extremism

Extremists increasingly use the Internet to further their ideology and promote radicalization. In a letter to the U.S. Senate Committee on Homeland Security and Governmental Affairs, Zachary Chesser (see details in "The Online Radicalization of Zachary Chesser" on page 8) said of the Internet, "It is simply the most dynamic and convenient form of media there is."[27] The convenience is due to the many ways in which the Internet can be used and from the perceived veil of anonymity under which extremists and consumers of extremist propa-ganda operate. Extremists use the Internet to provoke negative sentiment towards enemies, glorify martyrs,

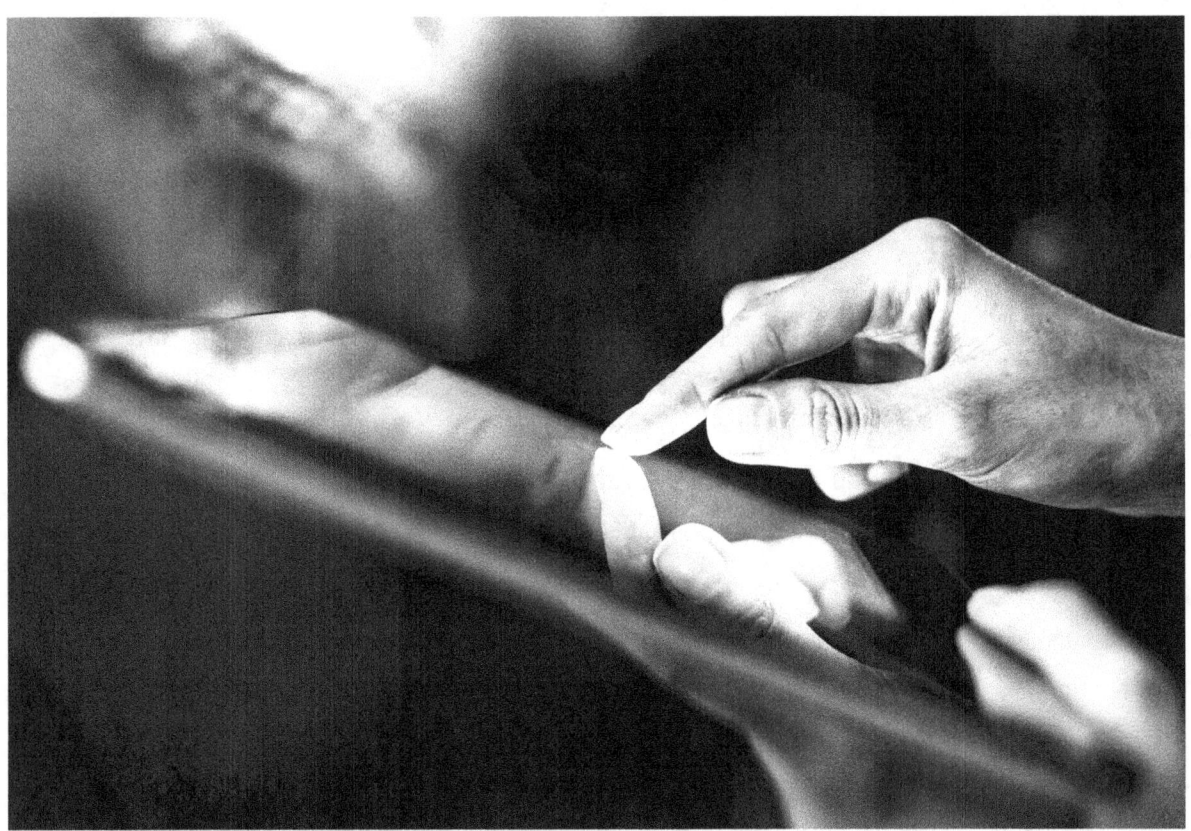

create virtual communities with like-minded individuals, provide religious or legal justifications for proposed actions, and communicate with and groom new recruits. Videos of successful attacks, lectures espousing radical views, blog posts, and messages encouraging attacks can also be posted online. Using a combination of traditional websites; mainstream social media platforms such as Facebook, Twitter, and YouTube; and other specialized sites, extremists are able to identify and groom potential recruits. This combination also allows for interaction with larger groups that would not otherwise be reached by conventional means, creating the appearance that extremist groups have critical mass. Violent extremists also use the Internet to incite people to violence and to post provocative materials such as educational videos about how to construct improvised explosive devices (IED) and operate weapons, essentially making it the new terrorist training ground. Overall, the Internet enables radicalization to occur in a virtual community, which also makes it harder for law enforcement to be aware of potential cases of radicalization to violence.

Extremists also use the Internet for purposes other than radicalization. Some groups use the Internet to raise money for their operations, to map out locations, and to practice with certain weapons and accessories. For example, Anders Breivik—the Norwegian responsible for killing 77 people and injuring more than 300 during sequential attacks on July 22, 2011—relied heavily on mapping sites to plan out his attacks and to identify locations to store weapons.[28] He also used first-person shooter games to practice with the weapon and sight he ultimately used during the attacks.[29] Sovereign citizens are also increasingly utilizing YouTube and other video-sharing sites to spread their message and highlight incidents in which their tactics were successful.

The Online Radicalization of Zachary Chesser

Zachary Chesser was an average high school student in northern Virginia. He participated in his high school's Gifted and Talented program, joined his high school break-dancing team, was an avid soccer player with aspirations of getting a scholarship to play in college, and worked part-time at a video rental store.

In the summer of 2008, 18-year-old Chesser converted to Islam and quickly became radicalized, solely on the Internet. He began posting views that supported Islamist terrorist groups, watching sermons by Anwar al Awlaki, and he exchanged emails with the cleric about joining Al Shabab. Within weeks, he had quit his job because he "objected to working at a place that rented videos featuring naked women" and became increasingly hostile to his parents.

By 2009, Chesser committed himself solely to using his computer and graphics skills to contribute to and promote violent extremist messages. He also attempted to travel to Somalia with his wife—whom he met through a series of comments on al Awlaki's blog— to join Al Shabab, but was unsuccessful when his mother-in-law hid his wife's passport. In 2010, he uploaded a video to YouTube, in which he threatened the creators of the television show *South Park* after an episode depicted the Prophet Muhammad dressed in a bear costume.

In July 2010, he attempted to join Al Shabab once again, but was held for questioning at the airport. A few days after being questioned, Chesser was arrested for attempting to provide material support to a terrorist organization. He pled guilty in October 2010 to three federal felony charges—communicating threats, soliciting violent jihadists to desensitize law enforcement, and attempting to provide material support to a designated foreign terrorist organization—and was sentenced in 2011 to 25 years in federal prison.*

---

* Majority and Minority Staff of the Senate Committee on Homeland Security and Governmental Affairs, *Zachary Chesser: A Case Study in Online Islamist Radicalization and Its Meaning for the Threat of Homegrown Terrorism* (Washington, DC: United States Senate, 2012).

KEY PRINCIPLES

"In the 21st Century the community policing philosophy is well positioned to take a central role in preventing and responding to terrorism and in efforts to reduce citizen fear." [30]

Community policing provides state, local, and tribal law enforcement agencies with the opportunity to build relationships with stakeholders across diverse communities. These relationships are most successful when founded on the principle that every interaction — whether made by a sworn officer, civilian, or volunteer — is treated as an opportunity to demonstrate the department's commitment to community policing and treat all community members with respect and equality. Successful partnerships allow agencies not only to better understand the needs and concerns of community members affected by the new role of law enforcement in countering violent extremism (CVE) initiatives but also to work together to address them. [31] Community policing also involves educating residents to recognize and report crimes and suspicious activities and empowering them to actively contribute to enhancing the safety of their neighborhoods. In addition to including residents, community policing provides ways for law enforcement to bring representatives from additional government agencies and community organizations and services to the table. Leveraging available resources from the community allows law enforcement to help mitigate the grievances that can lead to radicalization to violence and recruitment. Community policing principles have been used by many law enforcement agencies to address a host of crime and quality-of-life issues and can easily be repurposed to address CVE. The following key principles focus on how state, local, and tribal law enforcement agencies can continue to effectively deliver services and proactively respond to community concerns, while also addressing violent extremism of all types.

Key Principle #1: Foster and Enhance Trusting Partnerships with the Community

Partnerships and Community Policing

Trusting partnerships are the cornerstone of community policing. In order for these partnerships to be successful, they must be based on transparency, communication, and respect. Through communication and collaboration, law enforcement agencies and the people they serve can tailor initiatives to address specific, agreed-upon needs and help foster the common purpose of keeping communities safe. Working together to achieve these goals promotes mutual understanding that materializes as trust and enhances the partnerships. Especially in terms of countering violent extremism, trusting partnerships are necessary for law enforcement to achieve the appropriate balance between delivering traditional police services and working to prevent future attacks and for the community to feel comfortable about law enforcement. [32]

What Can My Agency Do?

Fostering trusting partnerships begins with being aware of community concerns and being sensitive to the norms and practices of diverse groups within the community. Taking into account specific tribal, religious, and social practices is essential for law enforcement when interacting and communicating with members of the community. Even within a specific group there may be different practices and beliefs that necessitate unique responses from law enforcement. For example, some religions prohibit traveling, eating, working, or answering phones and responding to emails on certain days. In some cultures it is preferable for female community members to interact with female officers and for men in the community to interact with male officers. Ensuring that officers are cognizant of these differences and prohibitions can go a long way in demonstrating the agency's willingness to partner with diverse groups to contribute to the safety of the community. This can include avoiding contacting certain individuals and scheduling community meetings on certain days. This understanding can also help officers distinguish between specific legal or constitutionally protected behaviors—such as speaking in a foreign language or praying—from suspicious activity or criminal behavior while also showing community members that law enforcement is committed to embracing them.

Communication is essential because it shapes how individuals view police agencies. Being honest, open, and transparent can solidify an agency's legitimacy in the community.[33] Communication must be balanced and information must be shared back and forth for the community to believe that law enforcement is interested in engaging them. In order to avoid being perceived as "securitizing the relationship," law enforcement agencies should share information about ongoing CVE initiatives with the community. To ensure that this information is disseminated to interested community members and organizations, agencies should have a single point of contact at each department substation responsible for taking calls and meeting with interested community members and organizations. This individual can also describe how information sharing, analysis, and dissemination occur within the agency. They can explain the applicable laws and protections that are afforded to people, identify who to contact if there are additional questions or concerns, and serve as a general resource for the community. That officer can also attend community events and prayer services or vigils in uniform. By attending these events in uniform, agencies can demonstrate their commitment to transparency in their CVE efforts and build trust with the community.

An important element of building trust with community members is being attuned to their perceptions of the balance between engagement efforts and gathering information and intelligence. Communities that believe law enforcement is only interested in collecting information and co-opting them into the intelligence gathering process—also known as "securitizing the relationship"—are more likely to feel alienated and less likely to work with law enforcement in the future. It is incumbent upon departments to separate any intelligence efforts from those related to outreach and engagement, to create or follow policies and procedures regarding information and tips received, and to be transparent with the community and educate them about all law enforcement efforts related to them.

For law enforcement to garner the respect of the community, it is imperative they treat every individual equally under the law. Every encounter and interaction between a community member and law enforcement—whether it be a sworn officer, civilian employee, or volunteer—must be conducted in a fair and equitable manner, must be done respectfully, and must be grounded in the principles of community policing. By demonstrating that the processes for responding to criminal incidents are equal regardless of race, religion, gender, or opinions and beliefs, law enforcement gains respect from all members of the community. As the most prevalent representative of government in the community, both sworn officers and civilian employees need to understand the importance of their actions whenever they interact with members of the community.

Trusting partnerships with community members will result from continued commitment to communication and transparency, collaboration, and respect. These partnerships will be focused on addressing and solving a broad array of concerns, including countering violent extremism. When community members trust officers enough to provide them with information about suspicious activities and trust that problems will be addressed in a cooperative manner, the legitimacy of that agency is solidified. This trust comes as a result of cooperation and open dialogue; transparency; protection of privacy, civil rights, and civil liberties; and continued commitment.[34]

Innovative Approaches

The Los Angeles Police Department (LAPD) Counter-Terrorism and Special Operations Bureau (CTSOB) Liaison Section was established to, "fully leverage the Department's public outreach capability and capacity in an effort to improve the quality of life and public safety within diverse communities by building mutual partnerships and trust."[35] Officers from the section were invited to participate in the Iranian New Year's "Fire Festival," in which people jump over fire to cleanse themselves of the past year and enter into the new one. Rather than simply attend the festival, officers joined in the tradition. The following year, officers repeated their attendance and participation. Additionally, a few years ago the LAPD held its first Chief's Muslim Community Forum, in an attempt to reach out to the large Muslim community. The meetings are now held quarterly at a variety of locations throughout the city, and Muslim leaders from across the greater Los Angeles area attend, demonstrating the importance of partnerships between law enforcement and the community.

The Loudoun County (Virginia) Sheriff's Office has one Community Resource Unit (CRU) at each station with a single deputy responsible for outreach and coordination of efforts with members of the community, business leaders, and homeowners' associations in their area.[36] These deputies also attend community events and make presentations at schools and places of worship throughout their jurisdictions. Deputies have conducted workshops for parents, students, teachers, religious leaders, and concerned community members. At each presentation, deputies provide their direct contact information, which ensures that community members who attend any of the meetings or events receive the same information. This engenders trust, because community members have the opportunity to become comfortable with the same individual over the years, and the deputy is able to form bonds with individuals and organizations that may not have been possible without such stability and consistency.

For the Montgomery County (Maryland) Police Department (MCPD), fostering and enhancing trusting relationships with community members comes as a result of being in the community and interacting with individuals on a regular basis. From the chief down to line officers, department representatives attend any events and meetings that they are invited to, in uniform, and establish relationships with attendees. By attending events in uniform, MCPD officers are able to distinguish themselves and to demonstrate the willingness of the department to work with members of the community. The distinction affords community members the ability to put faces and names to the badges and uniforms. This effectively humanizes the department and allows community members to see officers as more than enforcers of the law. In addition, the department provides training and information on a variety of subjects at the request of community members. For example, parents have asked for training about Internet safety for their children and immigrant groups have asked for information about community resources, both of which the department has provided. Attending community events and meetings in uniform and interacting with the hosts and attendees demonstrates the MCPD's commitment to fostering and enhancing trusting partnerships and shows the community that they too have a vested interest in creating a safe environment.

Key Principle #2: Engage All Residents to Address Public Safety Matters

Engagement and Community Policing

Under the community policing philosophy, all members of the community are viewed as partners who share responsibility for developing and implementing solutions to public safety priorities.[37] Inherent in this is the notion that individuals who live or work in a specific community are better situated to identify concerns and recognize suspicious activities.[38] Members of the community also have a vested interest in enhancing the safety of their neighborhood, but may be unaware of how to get involved. Therefore, it is important for law enforcement to build upon trusting partnerships with community members by reaching out to, and actively engaging, them in addressing public safety and quality-of-life matters.[39] Engaging everyone in the community can help contribute to its overall safety and help to prevent grievances that can lead to radicalization to violence and violent extremism.

What Can My Agency Do?

Law enforcement must reach out and engage each of the distinct sections of the community by providing them with information and education about the most prevalent concerns facing the community and how they can get involved. It is important for agencies to conduct this outreach in a manner that does not focus on certain individuals or groups at the expense of others or create the perception of profiling. In reaching out to various groups and subgroups, law enforcement may encounter people that are initially hesitant or unwilling to engage. Although it is easy to conclude that reluctance or resistance to engage means that they are uninterested, it should not be used as an excuse to dismiss or discredit their perspectives. In fact, resistance might not be lack of interest or motivation, but rather suspicion and mistrust based on previous interactions with, or assumptions of, law enforcement—either in the United States or abroad.[40] By engaging these individuals on a broad array of public safety and quality-of-life concerns, law enforcement can underscore that everyone has an important role to play in the safety of their community, and work to correct misperceptions about law enforcement.

In addition to talking to the community, law enforcement must listen to the community. This provides opportunities for law enforcement to learn from community members. Encouraging residents to voice their concerns and identify the priorities they would like to address can be more important than talking to them.

The perspectives of the community may be different than those of law enforcement and it is important for those differences to be heard and addressed by representatives on both sides. Additionally, affording the community opportunities to provide their own input fosters a sense of involvement in the policing process. Listening sessions can also provide communities opportunities to voice concerns regarding incidents in the news or names and acronyms of agency programs that may have caused unintentional repercussions.

Engaging all residents is especially important in countering violent extremism. Because of the widespread threat posed by the range of violent groups and the difficulties inherent in distinguishing who is a violent extremist or is on the path of radicalizing to violence, it can be easy for violent extremists to blend in to the community at large. There are no visual or physical cues—such as dress, location, or size—which automatically identify someone as a violent extremist to law enforcement. For instance, someone taking a picture may be plotting an attack, or they may be a tourist. However, community members are well-situated to help counter this "blend" factor by recognizing things that are out of the ordinary. By providing programs that engage the community and raise their awareness of potential indicators of radicalization to violence and of the different ways they can contact authorities to report such situations, the community can contribute to enhancing safety and violent extremists will have a more difficult time blending in to the population.

Civilians and volunteers within the department can provide law enforcement with valuable insight into ways to begin to reach out and engage the community. Civilian employees and volunteers live in the communities covered by the agency and may possess similar concerns or harbor similar grievances as others in the community. These individuals can also explain what motivated them to get involved, the steps they took to join the department, and the best ways to start reaching out to the community. Civilians and volunteers can also be leveraged as agency ambassadors in the community who can speak to the benefits of getting involved with law enforcement.[41] Advisory councils made up of community leaders and organizational partners that community members recognize and respect can also serve as valuable resources for engagement efforts at the grassroots level. These leaders and partners can serve as role models for community members and show the benefits of working with law enforcement. Law enforcement should also consider outreach to youth as a significant part of community engagement. Engaging them can help to lessen the impact of facilitators of radicalization, provide law enforcement with additional ideas about the best ways to reach other young people, and encourage them to be more civically active.

Law enforcement agencies can also engage and communicate with residents through social media. Agencies can post questions and encourage comments as a way to solicit tips and feedback and engage in dialogue with community members. Departments can also use their online presence to share flyers and information about upcoming community events, and encourage people to report any information they might have. Agencies can encourage residents to play an active role in addressing crime and disorder in their neighborhood by disseminating information about unsolved crimes and crime trends in the community on social media sites, effectively creating force multipliers. Social media can also be used to address violent extremism as part of a comprehensive approach to more traditional crimes. Explaining the potential roles that graffiti, identity theft, and counterfeiting can have in supporting terrorism can be accomplished through Facebook posts or YouTube videos. Engaging residents through social media empowers them to play active roles in making the community a safer place to live.

For more information about how law enforcement can use social media to engage community members, share information, and solicit tips, visit the IACP Center for Social Media at www.IACPSocialMedia.org.

Agencies can also complement their online engagement of residents by holding community or town hall meetings. These meetings can be held individually with separate groups or with the entire community at once. The community meetings should afford all individuals the opportunity to identify their concerns and ask any questions they have about the department and its initiatives. Chief executives and officers should understand that concerns and questions will cover a broad range of topics, including some that may not be related to law enforcement. After the concerns have been identified, law enforcement should explain to the community which concerns they can address and ways the community can help to address the priorities that serve the interests of all parties. This process can help identify how the community can get involved, help the community better understand the role of law enforcement, and help law enforcement better understand the concerns of the different groups in the community. Community members may also provide suggestions about the best ways to involve them, the most effective outreach methods, training and education programs on topics they are interested in, and potential solutions to problems. These meetings can spur community members to become more involved.

Citizen Police Academies (CPA), Police Reserves, and Explorer Posts are also valuable ways to engage community members. CPAs teach participants about public safety issues in their communities, the roles and challenges of law enforcement, and how community members can help. CPAs also provide individuals with an inside look at the functions, responsibilities, and operational procedures of law enforcement and provide residents the opportunity to interact with law enforcement and vice versa. Explorer Posts provide youth interested in law enforcement as a future career with the opportunity to engage with law enforcement and assist during police events and functions. These posts allow for law enforcement to engage individuals in enhancing the safety of the community while also providing these individuals the opportunity to learn more about law enforcement.

Innovative Approaches

In addition to conducting CPAs that are open to the community at large, the Hennepin County (Minnesota) Sheriff's Office (HCSO) provides group academies that are specifically adapted to certain ethnic and demographic groups. These one-day individual academies were suggested by an advisory group of community members as a way to better address the needs of specific members of the community. Though the general curriculum does not change, the HCSO tailors specific sections of the academies to the group's individual needs. The HCSO has held these one-day academies for youth, elders, and women. In some traditions women are discouraged from talking in the presence of men and also have a larger role in raising children. Therefore, during their one-day academy, no men are allowed. This allows the women to speak freely and ask specific questions regarding youth and what to do if they suspect their children are in a gang, may be using drugs or alcohol, or are missing. Other one-day academies are geared toward immigrant groups and offer language interpretation and culturally-specific public safety information. By holding these individual academies along with the general academy, the HCSO is able to better understand all of the members of the diverse communities that comprise Hennepin County.

The Dearborn (Michigan) Police Department (DPD) has a number of programs dedicated to community engagement, including a handful that are specifically intended for diverse youth. The DPD has a School Resource Officer (SRO) program, an Explorer program, and an internship program. An SRO is assigned to each public high school and also provides services to all of the elementary and middle schools in Dearborn. This program is intended to allow all youth—but specifically those who are first- or second-generation Americans—to become comfortable with law enforcement at an early age and to view them as educators and mentors instead of merely officers who enforce the law.[42] Dearborn also supports a Reserve Officer program and an Explorer program that expose youth in the city to the police department and profession. Both of these programs allow youth to serve as volunteers and assist in certain police functions, serve as liaisons in the community, and interact with employees throughout the DPD.[43] Many of the Reserve Officers and Explorers are youth from culturally diverse households. Finally, the DPD hires up to five high school students as interns, who are paid as well as offered college tuition reimbursement if they receive a degree related to law enforcement. The interns work alongside police officers and serve as ambassadors within both the community and the department. Each of these programs provides a means for youth to become engaged in the community and for the DPD to build inroads into the future of the community that can be leveraged to counter violent extremism.

Key Principle #3: Leverage Public and Private Stakeholders

Community Stakeholders and Community Policing

Partnerships with public and private stakeholders—such as other criminal justice agencies, government services, nonprofits, community organizations, private companies, and the media—can accomplish what individual community members or organizations and individual law enforcement agencies alone cannot by combining their distinct resources.[44] Leveraging the strengths of public and private stakeholders also connects individuals to available resources and services and increases public recognition and visibility of countering violent extremism (CVE) initiatives.

What Can My Agency Do?

Law enforcement agencies should partner with agencies and offices from across the criminal justice spectrum. Police departments can work with neighboring law enforcement agencies as part of a joint terrorism task force to share information about community concerns that cross jurisdictional lines and share leading community policing and countering violent extremism practices. Local law enforcement can also leverage their regional fusion centers, which conduct analysis of crime and threat-related information; facilitate information sharing between the Federal Government and state, local, and tribal law enforcement; assist law enforcement in preventing and responding to crime and extremism; and provide resources, training, and technical assistance to law enforcement. Because of the amount of information regional fusion centers have, they may be better positioned to provide an integrated view of suspicious activity reports and other information that could indicate radicalization to violence. Local agencies should also partner with sheriffs' offices to address the issues posed by sovereign citizens. Sovereigns recognize the sheriff as the highest law enforcement authority in the United States, and having the sheriff as a partner may help to quickly deescalate and avoid potential violence.

There are more than 70 state- and locally-run fusion centers across the United States. For more information about the fusion center closest to you, visit https://nfcausa.org/default. aspx/MenuItemID/117/MenuGroup/ Public+Home.htm.

In addition to law enforcement agencies, partnering with local courts should be considered. Sovereign citizens often attempt to seek revenge against individual law enforcement officers or their agency by filing liens and frivolous lawsuits, known as "paper terrorism."[45] By establishing a relationship with the county clerk, law enforcement can stay aware of any filings and take necessary measures to ensure that officers are protected. Law enforcement can also work cooperatively with corrections officials to ensure that those in custody are not subjected to recruitment by radicals; that religious needs—including dietary restrictions, prayer books, and services—are met; and that individuals being released have positive connections in the community.

Law enforcement agencies can also leverage faith- and community-based organizations and their leaders as valuable stakeholders in countering violent extremism. Community organizations such as nonprofits, service providers, and support groups can provide assistance to the community and advocate on its behalf.[46] These organizations often work with and are staffed by individuals who share commonalities with the people they represent. Therefore, they can be valuable partners in developing collaborative solutions to problems.[47] Similarly, faith-based organizations and their leaders address many of the same problems and provide indirect access to large subsets of the population. Distrust of law enforcement, language barriers, concerns about immigration status, and fear of deportation can affect partnership-building and engagement efforts. Faith- and community-based organizations generally have more experience addressing these concerns and helping individuals overcome them. They are well positioned to convey appropriate information to both the community and law enforcement and can serve as valuable intermediaries. Faith- and community-based organizations provide indirect access to large subsets of the population and provide law enforcement channels to disseminate information such as crime prevention tips, what to do if people witness a crime or are a victim, and numbers to contact if people have any questions. These organizations can also help identify individuals that either are at risk or have begun radicalizing so that interventions may occur before feelings of isolation set in. Religious leaders and leaders of community organizations can also provide strong examples to the community that seamless coexistence, religion and Western beliefs, and working with law enforcement can all happen and can contribute to the overall safety of the community.

Private businesses also have a large stake in the community and are important partners for law enforcement. Often, private businesses possess additional resources and have a vested interest in enhancing the safety of the community.[48] In addition to controlling a significant majority of the nation's infrastructure, businesses employ more people in private security than the number of people employed in state and local law enforcement.[49] Businesses also often have their own security technologies—such as closed circuit televisions and real-time alert systems—that can be instrumental to law enforcement. Businesses such as home-improvement companies, pharmacies, shipping companies, banks and money transfer companies, and private security companies can all serve as valuable partners. Home-improvement stores sell wires, pipes, nails, and fertilizer for legitimate purposes, but these are also common ingredients for IEDs. Pharmacies sell needles, medications, and chemicals that are intended to cure illnesses, but can also be used for illegitimate purposes. Banks and businesses that provide money transfers can be used to send money to extremists overseas. Even real estate agencies, tattoo artists, storage facilities, and rental car companies can come into contact with extremists prior to an attack.[50] Law enforcement can work with these different businesses to educate employees about certain indicators and how to recognize and report suspicious transactions or individuals. Providing this education can raise the awareness of the business community and help law enforcement receive valuable information even earlier in the process.

Finally, local media and affiliates for national outlets are important stakeholders for law enforcement to collaborate with. The media has an impact on public perceptions of the police and community concerns and can assist with publicizing CVE initiatives.[51] News stories and interviews with chief executives and community leaders about the benefits of collaborating and detailing successful engagement initiatives can present law enforcement and their efforts in a favorable light. These stories can also help alleviate some of the distrust and popular misconceptions about law enforcement and impress upon the community the need for continued vigilance and engagement. Working with the media can also be an effective way to share relevant information and maintain transparency regarding CVE initiatives. The media can increase public awareness of CVE initiatives by covering press conferences held by law enforcement and events cosponsored by law enforcement and the community. Coverage of these events allow people—who may have been hesitant to attend a live event where law enforcement would be present—to see other community members interacting with law enforcement in a positive way. This may help motivate them to attend future events and increase community engagement in CVE. Media personnel can also assist chief executives and public information officers with ways to best convey information to the public. This assistance can include tips about words and phrases to avoid in speeches and press releases.

There are also important officer safety implications that necessitate having strong working relationships with reliable media contacts. In some situations, broadcasts may unintentionally reveal locations and tactical movements of officers, potentially jeopardizing responses to ongoing situations. Additionally, media arriving at the scene of an incident may unknowingly block major access points for first responders and backup personnel. Having contacts that understand the gravity of these circumstances and that are accepting of officers' requests can be instrumental in ensuring the safety of everyone on scene without preventing the media from broadcasting important news.

Innovative Approaches

The Greensboro (North Carolina) Police Department (GPD) partners with personnel from across the spectrum of criminal justice and public safety to address problems posed by sovereign citizens in Guilford County and the City of Greensboro. When a sovereign citizen files a fraudulent lien or files a lawsuit against any employee of the GPD, the criminal justice system, or the local government, that information is relayed to the GPD immediately. The Guilford County Register of Deeds also notifies the GPD as soon as possible when it receives paperwork—whether it is a lien, lawsuit, or affidavit renouncing citizenship—filed by a sovereign citizen. Upon receiving such notifications, the GPD's Intelligence Squad sends a letter to the individual who filed the paperwork advising them that their filing is not legitimate. In some cases, the police attorney proactively sends letters to groups of sovereign citizens on behalf of the city's legal department indicating that if they ever anticipate filing a lawsuit or false lien the GPD will file a countersuit. The GPD also works with parking enforcement personnel on identifying illegal license plates belonging to sovereigns so that they can contact officers as soon as they see them. The department even partners with dispatchers to recognize keywords and catchphrases that are indicative of sovereign citizens so that they can relay that information to officers responding to calls for service or providing backup on traffic stops. By leveraging stakeholders from across the criminal justice and public safety realms, the GPD is able to ensure that any illegal endeavors by the sovereign citizen population are spearheaded as soon as possible.

In Boston, Massachusetts, the PortWatch program is a collaboration between public and private stakeholders to proactively address public safety and security concerns and raise security awareness in and around the Port of Boston. The program was established by the chief of the Massport Police (Massachusetts State Police, Troop F), who also serves as the director of maritime security for the Massachusetts Port Authority. The partnership uses the "Operation Cooperation" model developed by the IACP, the National Sheriffs' Association, and the American Society for Industrial Security. Partners include federal, state, and local law enforcement and regulatory agencies; private corporate security stakeholders and other private companies; and community representatives. These entities all share relevant information and intelligence, establish rapid response and layered response strategies, and provide operational support to one another. Information shared includes current trends in local, national, and international criminal or terrorist activity that may be relevant to the Port and its surrounding areas; upcoming significant events; and any operations that may impact daily routines. Law enforcement also works with private security directors to develop security awareness programs that are tailored to each company that is a part of the program. Additionally, PortWatch includes a training component, building on the federal "See Something, Say Something" campaign. Law enforcement partners teach employees of area hotels, restaurants, and other "soft targets" how to recognize and assess suspicious behaviors and what steps to take when reporting them to authorities. Together, the PortWatch program stakeholders are able to exchange relevant security information, educate the local community, and enhance the safety and security of the Port of Boston and surrounding communities.

For more information about "Operation Cooperation" visit www.ilj.org/publications/docs/ Operation_Cooperation.pdf.

The Montgomery County (Maryland) Police Department (MCPD) has strong working relationships with area media channels, which proved invaluable during a violent incident. On September 1, 2010, an environmental extremist entered the Discovery Channel headquarters wearing a vest that contained several bombs and holding two guns. The individual proceeded to hold two Discovery Communications employees and a security guard hostage for approximately four hours. As the MCPD and other local law enforcement officers and federal agents from the FBI and ATF responded to the scene, they were confronted with obstacles posed by the media. Despite law enforcement blocking off most of the streets around the building, helicopters from various news agencies hovered over the building broadcasting live. The footage included SWAT teams and off-duty officers that were establishing a perimeter around the building and setting up tactical positions. The MCPD explained that there were televisions in the lobby that the perpetrator could be using to watch the news and requested that the media ground its helicopters. Because of the strong partnerships and the explanation, the media outlets removed their helicopters from above the building. Similarly, a producer who called the building to get details about the ongoing situation had a brief telephone conversation with the perpetrator in which the perpetrator referenced his website and ideology. The producer notified authorities of the conversation and the MCPD requested that the producer not report the name of the perpetrator, the substance of the conversation, or that the conversation took place. This would prevent the perpetrator from getting the fame he sought and would not give him an opportunity to spread his propaganda. This request was also granted. As a result of the strong partnerships between the MCPD and the media, the police were able to avoid critical officer safety issues and avoid giving a violent extremist the notoriety he sought.

Key Principle #4: Utilize All Partnerships to Counter Violent Extremism

Putting Partnerships into Action

One of the goals of community policing is to provide communities with the support and resources they need to be able to uphold local safety and order as well as harness their own abilities to respond to emerging challenges.[52] Just as concerns and priorities are best identified by the community, responses that are developed and implemented by community members and stakeholders tend to be well-received and hold the most legitimacy. However, law enforcement should serve as an educator, facilitator, representative of local government, and resource provider. Agencies should educate community members and public and private stakeholders about the extremist threats facing them. They should also work cooperatively to enhance the capacity of the community to proactively arrive at solutions that counter these threats. With law enforcement serving in a supporting role, agencies can utilize all of their partners to create counter-narratives, build resilience, and counter violent

extremism. In fact, one of the objectives listed in the White House's *Strategic Implementation Plan for Empowering Local Partners to Prevent Violent Extremism in the United States* (SIP) is to "foster community-led partnerships and preventative programming to build resilience against violent extremist radicalization by expanding community-based solutions."[53]

Counter-narratives should provide clear, descriptive, and unbiased information that strategically counters the misleading and inciting propaganda proffered by extremists. The purpose of creating counter-narratives is to counter the ideologies and narratives that legitimize violence by standing for freedom, fairness, equality, dignity, hope, and opportunity, as well as affirming the ideals of inclusiveness and opportunity.[54] They can demonstrate that it is possible for ideology and citizenship to coexist in a peaceful manner and validate that the community will not accept violence of any type, especially violent extremism. Counter-narratives should be specific to the audience that is being addressed and should focus on the beliefs, ideas, and responses that are commonly held amongst these individuals. Depending on the audience, counter-narratives can take multiple forms—including pamphlets or booklets, posts or videos on social media sites, sermons or speeches, games, or physical demonstrations of unity throughout the community. It also means that certain counter-narratives may address violent extremism as an ancillary issue at first, while others directly address ideologies supported by extremist groups. There are no limits to how many counter-narratives a community can create or to the number of unique ways they can address threats facing different populations.

What Can My Agency Do?

In order for law enforcement to assist in the creation of an effective counter-narrative, agencies must understand the demographics of their community, the specific threats facing community members, and potential targets for extremists. Chief executives should ensure that they are aware of the different populations and groups in their area and of domestic and international situations that could have local repercussions and should conduct threat assessments of potential targets in their area. Chief executives should disseminate all information they've gathered throughout the department so that every employee and volunteer has a working knowledge of the communities they serve and potential issues that may arise when responding to calls for service or requests from community members. This is especially important for agencies that have sizeable immigrant or refugee populations, because perceptions of law enforcement can be shaped as much by the country of origin as by U.S. values and institutions. In turn, officers can use the necessary information to assist the community in identifying and understanding the threats that face them specifically. Officers should also address any popular misconceptions about the threats, violent extremism, and radicalization. Law enforcement must ensure that the community understands that specific groups or races should not be discriminated against or targeted based on the actions of a few individuals. Educating the community will enable the community to formulate appropriate measures to take to ensure their own safety and to create an appropriate counter-narrative.

One of the byproducts of providing the information necessary for the community to create their own counter-narratives is the fostering of a resilient community. Resilience is defined as the process shaped by resources—such as economic development, social capital, information and communication, and community competence—that may lead to adaptation after a disturbance or adversity.[55] Simply stated, it is the ability to resist, absorb, recover from, or successfully adapt to adversity or a change in conditions.[56] In terms of countering violent extremism, resilience is the ability of the community to stand up against extremist recruiters and to quickly coordinate a response should an attack occur.

Resilience consists of a combination of individual and social characteristics that include family, community, society, state, and global dynamics. Family and societal ties are the strongest elements of resilience. Family members are the first to notice behavioral changes that may indicate radicalization to violence. Participation in community groups and events can create positive social ties for individuals that may have otherwise been at risk. Just as with the creation of counter-narratives, resilience is best cultivated by the community itself. Law enforcement's role in building resilience should consist of identifying existing resources that are available for individuals and groups, and opportunities for community members to get engaged.

Innovative Approaches

A controversial pastor planned a student walkout in protest of alleged bullying of non-Muslim students by Muslim students at a school in Dearborn, Michigan. Though the planned walkout was nonviolent and the pastor only intended to express views protected by the First Amendment, the city came together to ensure that the demonstration was a non-event. The Dearborn Police Department (DPD) worked with other law enforcement agencies, city and school officials and security staff, the Dearborn Area Ministerial Alliance (DAMA), Ford Motor Company, and parents and community volunteers to prepare. The DPD began planning for the demonstration weeks before it was scheduled to occur.[57] The DPD, school officials, and city officials also held meetings days before the demonstration to educate parents about the steps the city was taking to respond to the demonstration, traffic control around the school, and the importance of sending children to school as a sign that the community would not be intimidated by the controversial pastor.[58] The DPD also met with city officials and the DAMA before the rally to ask that the religious leaders suggest that their congregants not attend or respond with violence. One of the churches was also used as a media staging area during the demonstration. The Michigan State Police, the Wayne County Sheriff's Office, federal partners, and school district security personnel were also present at the school more than an hour before the demonstration was set to begin to assist the DPD.[59] These officials helped set up barriers approximately 25 yards from school property and kept protestors on the sidewalks because they did not have a permit to be on school grounds. The demonstration proved to be uneventful because none of the students the pastor was hoping to enlist joined in and only a handful of protestors attended. Engaging a wide array of partners, the DPD and the Dearborn community used community policing principles and techniques to successfully demonstrate their resilience.

Key Principle #5: Train All Members of the Department

Training and Community Policing

At its most fundamental level, violent extremism should be treated as another violent crime that community policing can be used to alleviate. Training programs should get to the root of community policing and encourage a proactive and collaborative approach to responding to concerns identified by the community, communicating through a variety of different methods, and applying analytical skills.[60] Training should also concentrate on important operational elements of community policing such as the value of building and maintaining partnerships, the importance of being respectful and fair at all times, and the significance of being the face of the department and the government liaison in every encounter. Training modules should also cover how these elements of community policing can be integrated with homeland security. These modules can focus on repurposing resources and personnel and applying them in ways that support the shift from a reactive model of responding to calls for service to a proactive model. Modules can also focus on the systematic use of partnerships, initiatives for building community resilience, and maximizing resources already available in the community to counter violent extremism.[61]

What Can My Agency Do?

Training modules specifically related to community policing and countering violent extremism (CVE) should cover topics including civil liberties and relevant protections, cultural awareness and sensitivity, outreach, and information sharing. According to the White House's *Strategic Implementation Plan for Empowering Local Partners to Prevent Violent Extremism in the United States* (SIP), training that addresses these topics is critical so that "the Federal Government and its local government and law enforcement partners understand what the threat of violent extremism is, and what it is not."[62] This highlights the fact that one of the most important things is to distinguish constitutionally protected behaviors from suspicious activities and violent extremism. Basic cultural awareness training is imperative for all law enforcement agencies. Training should provide overviews of important information (e.g., holidays and practices for all religions; popular misconceptions and misperceptions) and identify community individuals and resources where more information can be found and questions can be answered.

It is important that all training be unbiased, accurate, and up to date. Agencies should reach out to respected community leaders and organizations to see if they are interested in providing training. This can afford the community the opportunity to highlight practices that are most important to them and the best ways law enforcement can respond. Community leaders may also appreciate the opportunity to answer questions and address misperceptions. If community leaders are unable to provide cultural awareness training, consulting them in choosing trainers can help ensure that self-proclaimed subject matter experts are avoided. Training that is biased or contains inaccurate information can impact the willingness of individuals to cooperate with law enforcement, may further grievances, and can be leveraged by extremist recruiters to support their narrative and radicalize individuals. It can also be used to file complaints or lawsuits against the department. However, when employees are properly trained to recognize and understand common behaviors and languages that they are likely to encounter, they are better able to respond appropriately and make informed decisions.[63] These measured responses and informed decisions will manifest themselves during interactions with the community and can solidify the legitimacy of law enforcement in the eyes of the community. Furthermore, agency employees that are trained and equipped to identify suspicious behaviors and individuals can be invaluable assets in efforts to counter violent extremism before an attack occurs.[64]

Law enforcement agencies should also train employees on the importance of separating the gathering of information and intelligence from outreach and engagement efforts. While a single agency can have separate units that are responsible for intelligence and outreach, it is imperative that they remain separate. Agencies must understand that they play an integral role in maintaining the delicate balance that exists between collecting information and maintaining a safe community and that counterterrorism and countering violent extremism must never be used interchangeably. In order to ensure that these two distinct functions never overlap, departments must follow—or establish—policies and procedures and provide training on the roles and responsibilities of all employees. Training on this topic can include the roles and responsibilities of all levels of employees, what to do with information and tips provided by community members, how information should be passed on, and who will be responsible for following up with those individuals who provided information, as well as any additional steps necessary. For agencies that either participate in a joint terrorism task force (JTTF) that gathers active intelligence or receive information, intelligence, analysis, or other reports from fusion centers, training should also cover policies and procedures related to gathering and sharing such information.

Regardless of the type of training provided, it should be mandatory for all agency employees—both sworn and civilian—and should be open to volunteers as well. The training curricula should be tailored to the different types of personnel. For example, training for line officers should emphasize that their individual actions have larger ramifications for both the department and law enforcement as a whole. With individuals increasingly able to record interactions with law enforcement, officers should be trained to understand that the eyes of the public are always open. Training for analysts should focus on the importance of exercising caution when using certain words and phrases. Analysts should be instructed to avoid using phrases that could be interpreted as insensitive or perceived as a front for gathering intelligence. Dispatchers should be trained to recognize indicators that may be important to relay to officers responding to a call for service. Similarly, civilians and volunteers that may provide follow-up services on behalf of an agency should be provided cultural awareness and sensitivity training. These training modules should require employees to sign off that they have participated, completed, and understood all aspects of the training. This demonstrates the importance of the material and solidifies the department's commitment to successfully implementing community policing principles to counter violent extremism.

Innovative Approaches

The Los Angeles Police Department (LAPD) and the Los Angeles County Sheriff's Department (LASD) provide officers and deputies with some of the most comprehensive CVE training. All LAPD officers and LASD deputies are trained as Terrorism Liaison Officers in Basic and Intermediary capacities. Officers and deputies attend courses on criminal networks as they pertain to terrorism and money laundering schemes, as well as other courses related to prevalent extremist ideologies. LAPD officers also attend trainings presented by the LASD, and vice versa, in order to conduct critical analyses to help eliminate any inflammatory material and damaging instruction being taught about certain religions and individuals. The two agencies partnered with the Muslim Public Affairs Council to develop a training video for officers and deputies regarding Muslim contacts. In addition, all recruits must complete cultural competency courses that cover cultural sensitivities, common greetings in different languages, key principles and promising practices for law enforcement, and differences between religions and sects of the same religion. The LAPD has even partnered with regional representatives of the Anti-Defamation League to ensure that all of the training modules are developed with civil rights and civil liberties in mind.

The Royal Canadian Mounted Police (RCMP) provides a cross-cultural awareness training program to employees who are stationed in communities with diverse ethnic populations. Called the National Security Cultural Awareness Training Course, it is the result of collaborative efforts between these communities and the RCMP to enhance cultural competency and maintain operational effectiveness. The core of the training program is consistent for employees throughout the nation, but there is significant flexibility built in to allow for input from community leaders in each of the communities. These leaders include information about the geopolitical context, how global trends affect communities in Canada, and practices and customs that are specific to their community and are most important for law enforcement to be aware of. Site visits to places of worship are also conducted to further enhance law enforcement's understanding of the community and to build networks with attendees. In many cases, the community leaders also deliver the training. The training program demystifies many myths and stereotypes, allows for open and honest dialogue between law enforcement and community leaders on sensitive issues, and provides employees with valuable training specific to their jurisdiction.

Finally, a number of Federal Government agencies have also been tasked with creating training programs and curricula related to countering violent extremism. The U.S. Department of Homeland Security (DHS), in partnership with the Federal Bureau of Investigation (FBI) and the IACP, launched a Countering Violent Extremism (CVE) Training Resource web portal on the Homeland Security Information Network. The purpose of the portal is to provide law enforcement agencies with the most current CVE training materials, case studies, analytic products, and other resources.[65] The COPS Office also provides "comprehensive and innovative education, training, and technical assistance to state, local, and tribal law enforcement" on community policing and emerging law enforcement topics including homeland security.[66] One of the courses the COPS Office funds, provided by the Virginia Center for Policing Innovation, is Tactical Community Policing for America's Homeland Security (TCPHS) Initiatives.[67] TCPHS focuses on enhancing the capacity of law enforcement to partner with relevant stakeholders on homeland security initiatives and to integrate homeland roles with community policing responsibilities.

CONCLUSION

"And so we must defeat determined enemies, wherever they are, and build coalitions that cut across lines of region and race and religion. And America's moral example must always shine for all who yearn for freedom and justice and dignity."[68]

In the years since 9/11, the law enforcement community has been faced with credible threats of violent extremism from an ever-evolving collection of determined enemies from overseas and within the United States. While terrorism remains a real and persistent problem—and the changing nature of the threat has made the chances of a successful attack more likely—law enforcement agencies have continually risen to the challenge. Whether the threats have come from international terrorist organizations, domestic extremist groups, or homegrown violent extremists, law enforcement has made considerable progress in developing methods and strategies for proactively detecting and thwarting new plots.

One of the most important strategies has been the repurposing and refining of community oriented policing practices. Law enforcement agencies have used these practices for decades to address other criminal and quality-of-life issues, such as gang violence and vandalism, and are now using them to address CVE. State, local, and tribal law enforcement agencies are focusing on fostering and enhancing partnerships with the community, building trust, using a whole-of-community approach, engaging the community, assisting with the creation of counter-narratives, helping build resilient communities, balancing engagement and information gathering, and training officers with special focus on preventing extremist attacks and reducing the number of individuals who radicalize to violence.

The marriage of community policing and countering violent extremism leverages the most valuable resource of each: local communities and their members. Law enforcement is empowering communities to impress upon individuals that everyone has an important role to play in the community. While radicalization to violence is occurring in homes across the country, thanks in large part to the Internet, community policing is being used to reach out to disenfranchised individuals and redirect them from the path of radicalization to violence. Community members are being invited to teach law enforcement about their religion, culture, and beliefs, so that officers are able to identify specific legal or constitutionally protected behaviors and not mistake those practices for criminal behavior. Community members are being encouraged to report suspicious activities, and communities are being empowered to demonstrate that they are stronger than the virtual community and that freedom, justice, and dignity can coexist with religion, culture, and citizenship.

Community policing is also best positioned to achieve the dual goals of protecting communities from attacks and protecting civil rights and liberties. The moral example set by the freedoms in the Constitution must never be outshined by suspicion or the desire to silence ideologies that are not considered mainstream. The freedoms of speech, press, religion, and assembly should never be repressed because they are perceived to be violent or offensive. The Law Enforcement Oath of Honor includes the commitment to "always uphold the Constitution," and that must remain true regardless of the circumstance.

ENDNOTES

1. *Empowering Local Partners to Prevent Violent Extremism in the United States* (Washington, DC: The White House, 2011), http://www.whitehouse.gov/sites/default/files/empowering_local_partners.pdf.
2. Michael Wagers, "Protecting the Homeland: Focusing on Prevention and State, Local, and Tribal Law Enforcement," *The Police Chief* 79 (February 2012): 20–21, http://www.policechiefmagazine.org/magazine/index.cfm?fuseaction=display_arch&article_id=2598&issue_id=22012.
3. *From Hometown Security to Homeland Security: IACP's Principles for a Locally Designed and Nationally Coordinated Homeland Security Strategy* (Alexandria, VA: International Association of Chiefs of Police, 2005), http://www.theiacp.org/portals/0/pdfs/HomelandSecurityWP.pdf.
4. Kim Morava, "Trooper Who Arrested Timothy McVeigh Shares Story," *The Shawnee News-Star,* February 25, 2009, http://www.news-star.com/article/20090225/NEWS/302259941.
5. Ibid.
6. *Community Policing Defined* (Washington, DC: Office of Community Oriented Policing Services, 2012), http://ric-zai-inc.com/Publications/cops-p157-pub.pdf.
7. Ibid., 3.
8. Ibid., 5.
9. Ibid., 10.
10. Matthew C. Scheider, Robert E. Chapman, and Michael F. Seelman, "Connecting the Dots for a Proactive Approach," *Border and Transportation Security* (2004): 158–162, http://ric-zai-inc.com/Publications/cops-w0245-pub.pdf.
11. Ibid., 162.
12. Barack Obama, "Remarks by the President in State of Union Address" (State of the Union Address, Washington, DC, January 25, 2011), http://www.whitehouse.gov/the-press-office/2011/01/25/remarks-president-state-union-address.
13. Pradine Saint-Forth, Noelle Yasso, and Susan Shah, *Engaging Police in Immigrant Communities* (Washington, DC: Office of Community Oriented Policing Services, 2012), http://www.vera.org/pubs/engaging-police-immigrant-communities-promising-practices-field.
14. "Homeland Security through Community Policing," Office of Community Oriented Policing Services, http://www.cops.usdoj.gov/Default.asp?Item=2472.
15. Mark F. Guiliano, "The Post 9/11 FBI: The Bureau's Response to Evolving Threats" (speech, Washington Institute for Near East Policy, Stein Program on Counterterrorism and Intelligence, Washington, D.C., April 14, 2011), http://www.fbi.gov/news/speeches/the-post-9-11-fbi-the-bureaus-response-to-evolving-threats.
16. Gary LaFree, Laura Dugan, and Erin Miller, *Integrated United States Security Database (IUSSD): Data on the Terrorist Attacks in the United States Homeland, 1970 to 2011—Final Report to Resilient Systems Division, DHS Science and Technology Directorate, U.S. Department of Homeland Security* (College Park, MD: National Consortium for the Study of Terrorism and Responses to Terrorism [START], 2012), http://www.start.umd.edu/sites/default/files/files/publications/START_IUSSDDataTerroristAttacksUS_1970-2011.pdf.
17. Ibid., 26.
18. *A Common Lexicon* (Alexandria, VA: International Association of Chiefs of Police, 2011), http://www.theiacp.org/portals/0/pdfs/IACP-COT_CommonLexicon_Eng_FINALAug12.pdf.
19. Brian Mitchell Jenkins, *Stray Dogs and Virtual Armies: Radicalization and Recruitment to Jihadist Terrorism in the United States Since 9/11* (Santa Monica, CA: RAND Corporation, 2011), www.rand.org/content/dam/rand/pubs/occasional_papers/2011/RAND_OP343.pdf.
20. *Foreign Fighters* (Alexandria, VA: International Association of Chiefs of Police, 2011), http://www.theiacp.org/portals/0/pdfs/IACP-COT_ForeignFighters__FINALAug12.pdf.
21. *A Common Lexicon* (see note 18).
22. Thom Jackson, "Officer Safety Corner: Sovereign Citizens on Traffic Stops," *The Police Chief* 80 (February 2013): 14–15, http://www.policechiefmagazine.org/magazine/index.cfm?fuseaction=display&article_id=2862&issue_id=22013.
23. Ibid., 14.
24. LaFree, Dugan, and Miller, *Integrated United States Security Database* (see note 16).
25. Lauren B. O'Brien, "The Evolution of Terrorism Since 9/11," *FBI Law Enforcement Bulletin: Terrorism* 80, no. 9 (2011), 3–10, http://www.fbi.gov/stats-services/publications/law-enforcement-bulletin/september-2011/September-2011-leb.pdf.
26. *A Common Lexicon* (see note 18).
27. Majority and Minority Staff of the Senate Committee on Homeland Security and Governmental Affairs, *Zachary Chesser: A Case Study in Online Islamist Radicalization and Its Meaning for the Threat of Homegrown Terrorism* (Washington, DC: United States Senate, 2012), http://www.hsgac.senate.gov/imo/media/doc/CHESSER%20FINAL%20REPORT%281%29.pdf.

28. Jacob Aasland Ravndal, "A Post-Trial Profile of Anders Behring Breivik," *CTC Sentinel* 5, no. 10 (October 2012): 16–20, https://www.ctc.usma.edu/wp-content/uploads/2012/10/CTCSentinel-Vol5Iss104.pdf.

29. Ibid., 17.

30. Scheider, Chapman, and Seelman, "Connecting the Dots," (see note 10).

31. Heather J. Davies and Gerard R. Murphy, *Protecting Your Community from Terrorism, Volume 2: Working with Diverse Communities* (Washington, DC: Office of Community Oriented Policing Services, 2004), http://ric-zai-inc.com/Publications/cops-w0168-pub.pdf.

32. Ibid., 2.

33. Edward Maguire and William Wells, introduction to *Implementing Community Policing: Lessons from 12 Agencies* (Washington, DC: Office of Community Oriented Policing Services, 2009), http://ric-zai-inc.com/Publications/cops-p172-pub.pdf.

34. Tammy A. Rinehart, Anna T. Laszlo, and Gwen O. Briscoe, *The COPS Collaboration Toolkit: How to Build, Fix and Sustain Productive Partnerships* (Washington, DC: Office of Community Policing Services, 2005), http://ric-zai-inc.com/Publications/cops-cd019-pub.pdf.

35. Los Angeles Police Department and Los Angeles County Sheriff's Department, "IACP and Booz Allen Hamilton Outstanding Achievement in the Prevention of Terrorism Award" (award application, 2011).

36. "Community Resource Unit," Loudoun County Sheriff's Office, http://sheriff.loudoun.gov

37. Scheider, Chapman, and Seelman, "Connecting the Dots," (see note 10).

38. *Community Policing Defined* (see note 6).

39. Gayle Fisher-Stewart, *Community Policing Explained: A Guide for Local Governments* (Washington, DC: Office of Community Oriented Policing Services, 2007), http://ric-zai-inc.com/Publications/cops-p136-pub.pdf.

40. Maguire and Wells, introduction to *Implementing Community Policing* (see note 33).

41. Ibid., 142.

42. Ronald Haddad, "Building Trust, Driving Relationships with the Dearborn, Michigan Arab American Community," *The Police Chief* 78 (March 2011): 42–47, http://www.policechiefmagazine.org/magazine/index.cfm?fuseaction=display_arch&article_id=2335&issue_id=32011.

43. Ibid., 46–47.

44. *Community Policing Defined* (see note 6).

45. Daniel Leaderman, "'Sovereign Citizens' Reject the System, but Use It against You," *The Gazette*, June 14, 2013, http://www.gazette.net/article/20130614/NEWS/130619445/-1/-x2018-sovereign-citizens-x2019-reject-the-system-but-use-it&template=gazette.

46. *Community Policing Defined* (see note 6).

47. Ibid., 3.

48. Ibid., 3.

49. *National Policy Summit: Building Private Security/Public Policing Partnerships to Prevent and Respond to Terrorism and Public Disorder* (Washington, DC: Office of Community Oriented Policing Services, 2005), http://ric-zai-inc.com/Publications/cops-w0704-pub.pdf.

50. "Homeland Security Publications," Ohio Homeland Security, http://www.homelandsecurity.ohio.gov/printed_material.stm.

51. *Community Policing Defined* (see note 6).

52. Maguire and Wells, introduction to *Implementing Community Policing* (see note 33).

53. *Strategic Implementation Plan for Empowering Local Partners to Prevent Violent Extremism in the United States* (Washington, DC: The White House, 2011), http://www.whitehouse.gov/sites/default/files/sip-final.pdf.

54. Ibid.

55. Stevan Weine and Osman Ahmed, *Building Resilience to Violent Extremism Among Somali-Americans in Minneapolis-St. Paul, Final Report to Human Factors/Behavioral Sciences Division, Science and Technology Directorate, U.S. Department of Homeland Security* (College Park, MD: National Consortium for the Study of Terrorism and Responses to Terrorism [START], 2012), http://www.start.umd.edu/sites/default/files/files/publications/Weine_BuildingResiliencetoViolentExtremism_SomaliAmericans.pdf.

56. Homeland Security Advisory Council, *Community Resilience Task Force Recommendations* (Washington, DC: U.S. Department of Homeland Security, 2011), www.dhs.gov/xlibrary/assets/hsac-community-resilience-task-force-recommendations-072011.pdf.

57. Joe Slezak, "Dearborn: School, City Officials Take Terry Jones' Appearance Outside School Seriously," *Press and Guide*, October 22, 2012, http://www.pressandguide.com/articles/2012/10/22/news/doc507f2232b9103090331097.txt?viewmode=fullstory

58. Ibid.

59. Ibid.

60. Ibid.

61. *Community Policing Defined* (see note 6).

62. *Strategic Implementation Plan* (see note 53).

63. Saint-Forth, Yasso, and Shah, *Engaging Police in Immigrant Communities* (see note 13).

64. Walter A. McNeil, "Homeland Security Is Hometown Security," *The Police Chief* 79 (February 2012), http://www.police-chiefmagazine.org/magazine/index.cfm?fuseaction=display_arch&article_id=2593&issue_id=22012.

65. "The Role of Community Policing in Homeland Security and Preventing Radicalization to Violence," International Association of Chiefs of Police, http://www.theiacp.org/CVE.

66. "Training," Office of Community Oriented Policing Services, http://www.cops.usdoj.gov/Default.asp?Item=1974.

67. "Community Policing Training and Technical Assistance," Office of Community Oriented Policing Services, http://www.cops.usdoj.gov/Default.asp?Item=2624.

68. Obama, "Remarks by the President" (see note 12).

ABOUT THE IACP

The International Association of Chiefs of Police (IACP) is the world's premier law enforcement membership organization, dedicated to serving the leaders of today and developing the leaders of tomorrow. The IACP was founded in 1893 to encourage cooperation and exchange of information among police administrators and to promote the highest standards of performance and conduct within the police profession. With more than 23,000 members in more than 100 countries, this vision continues today.

The IACP serves the leaders of today through advocacy, education, research, and professional services. From new technologies to emerging threats and trends, the IACP is at forefront of the most contemporary and pressing issues facing police leaders. Through internationally acclaimed conferences and trainings, ground-breaking research, and unparalleled outreach and advocacy efforts, the IACP works hard to help law enforcement respond to these issues.

The IACP is also focused on developing the leaders of tomorrow. The IACP Center for Police Leadership, Police Chief Mentoring program, and Discover Policing initiative are just a few examples of the many training and educational opportunities designed to prepare tomorrow's leaders for the challenges they will face.

Learn more at www.theiacp.org

ABOUT THE COPS OFFICE

The Office of Community Oriented Policing Services (COPS Office) is the component of the U.S. Department of Justice responsible for advancing the practice of community policing by the nation's state, local, territory, and tribal law enforcement agencies through information and grant resources.

Community policing is a philosophy that promotes organizational strategies that support the systematic use of partnerships and problem-solving techniques, to proactively address the immediate conditions that give rise to public safety issues such as crime, social disorder, and fear of crime.

Rather than simply responding to crimes once they have been committed, community policing concentrates on preventing crime and eliminating the atmosphere of fear it creates. Earning the trust of the community and making those individuals stakeholders in their own safety enables law enforcement to better understand and address both the needs of the community and the factors that contribute to crime.

The COPS Office awards grants to state, local, territory, and tribal law enforcement agencies to hire and train community policing professionals, acquire and deploy cutting-edge crime fighting technologies, and develop and test innovative policing strategies. COPS Office funding also provides training and technical assistance to community members and local government leaders and all levels of law enforcement. The COPS Office has produced and compiled a broad range of information resources that can help law enforcement better address specific crime and operational issues, and help community leaders better understand how to work cooperatively with their law enforcement agency to reduce crime.

- Since 1994, the COPS Office has invested more than $14 billion to add community policing officers to the nation's streets, enhance crime fighting technology, support crime prevention initiatives, and provide training and technical assistance to help advance community policing.
- To date, the COPS Office has funded approximately 125,000 additional officers to more than 13,000 of the nation's 18,000 law enforcement agencies across the country in small and large jurisdictions alike.
- Nearly 700,000 law enforcement personnel, community members, and government leaders have been trained through COPS Office-funded training organizations.
- To date, the COPS Office has distributed more than 8.57 million topic-specific publications, training curricula, white papers, and resource CDs.

COPS Office resources, covering a wide breadth of community policing topics—from school and campus safety to gang violence—are available, at no cost, through its online Resource Center at www.cops.usdoj.gov This easy-to-navigate website is also the grant application portal, providing access to online application forms.